I Help on Our Farm

Jamie Holloway

Rosen REAL READERS

Rosen Classroom
New York

I help feed the calves.

I help move the hay.

I help plant the carrots.

I help water the plants.

I help pick the carrots and kale.

I help pick the apples.

Words To Know

apples

calves

hay

kale